YOUR KNOWLEDGE HA

Bibliographic information published by the German National Library:

The German National Library lists this publication in the National Bibliography; detailed bibliographic data are available on the Internet at http://dnb.dnb.de .

Imprint:

Copyright © 2018 GRIN Verlag
Print and binding: Books on Demand GmbH, Norderstedt Germany
ISBN: 9783668722187

This book at GRIN:

https://www.grin.com/document/428121

Shahriat Hossain, Kh Ashique Mahmud

The pros and cons of modern web application security flaws and possible solutions

GRIN Verlag

GRIN - Your knowledge has value

Since its foundation in 1998, GRIN has specialized in publishing academic texts by students, college teachers and other academics as e-book and printed book. The website www.grin.com is an ideal platform for presenting term papers, final papers, scientific essays, dissertations and specialist books.

Visit us on the internet:

http://www.grin.com/

http://www.facebook.com/grincom

http://www.twitter.com/grin_com

THE PROS AND CONS OF MODERN WEB APPLICATION SECURITY FLAWS AND
POSSIBLE SOLUTIONS

Authors: Shahriat Hossain, Kh Ashique Mahmud

August 2018

Master of Computer Science

University of South Asia

Department of Computer Science and Engineering

Abstract:

Modern web applications have higher user expectations and greater demands than ever before. The security of these applications is no longer optional; it has become an absolute necessity. Web applications contain vulnerabilities, which may lead to serious security flaws such as stealing of confidential information. To protect against security flaws, it is important to understand the detailed steps of attacks and the pros and cons of existing possible solutions. The goal of this paper is to research modern web application security flaws and vulnerabilities. It then describes steps by steps possible approaches to mitigate them.

Acknowledgements:

We would like to thank everyone who has contributed in some way to this work.

Firstly, we would like to thank USA and its staff for making this learning experience possible. We would like to specially acknowledge all the lecturers and assistants who have participated in different courses of the MSc. Computer Science Program, including the students I've had the opportunity to work with. The diversity of backgrounds and the participation of both on-campus and distance students have made this learning journey very enriching.

Secondly, we would like to express our sincere gratitude to Md. Tomig Uddin Ahmed for being the supervisor of this work.

Lastly, we would like to thank my family for their support and especially recognize our friends Abdullah and Emran Karim for their interesting comments and discussions.

Table of Contents

1. INTRODUCTION:

Web applications are computer programs those utilize web browsers and web technology to form tasks over the Internet [13].

Figure-1: How web application works

Millions of businesses use the Internet as a cost-effective communications channel. It lets them exchange information with their target market and make fast, secure transactions. However, effective engagement is only possible when the business is able to capture and store all the necessary data, and have a means of processing this information and presenting the results to the user.

Web applications use a combination of server-side scripts (PHP and ASP) to handle the storage and retrieval of the information, and client-side scripts (JavaScript and HTML) to present information to users. This allows users to interact with the company using online forms, content management systems, shopping carts and more. In addition, the applications allow employees to create documents, share information, collaborate on projects, and work on common documents regardless of location or device.

Web applications must be secure, flexible, and scalable to meet spikes in demand. [14] As with any new class of technology, web applications have brought with them a new range of security vulnerabilities. The set of most commonly encountered defects has evolved somewhat over time. New attacks have been conceived that were not considered when existing applications were developed. Some problems have become less prevalent as awareness of them has increased. New technologies have been developed that have introduced new possibilities for exploitation. Some categories of flaws have largely gone away as the result of changes made to web browser software.

[14] The most serious attacks against web applications are those that expose sensitive data or gain unrestricted access to the back-end systems on which the application is running. High-profile compromises of this kind continue to occur frequently. For many organizations, however, any attack that causes system downtime is a critical event. Application-level denial-of-service attacks can be used to achieve the same results as traditional resource exhaustion attacks against infrastructure. However, they are often used with more subtle techniques and objectives. They may be used to disrupt a

particular user or service to gain a competitive edge against peers in the realms of financial trading, gaming, online bidding, and ticket reservations.

Throughout this evolution, compromises of prominent web applications have remained in the news. There is no sense that a corner has been turned and that these security problems are on the wane. By some measure, web application security is today the most significant battleground between attackers and those with computer resources and data to defend, and it is likely to remain so for the foreseeable future.

In particular, this topic focuses on 10 modern and significant web security pitfalls to be aware of, including recommendations on how they can be mitigated. The focus is on the **Top 10 Web Vulnerabilities [1]** identified by the **Open Web Application Security Project (OWASP)**, an international, non-profit organization whose goal is to improve software security across the globe.

2. BACKGROUND:

Insecure web application is undermining our financial, healthcare, defense, energy, and other critical infrastructure. As our application becomes increasingly complex, and connected, the difficulty of achieving application security increases exponentially. The rapid pace of modern web application development processes makes the most common risks essential to discover and resolve quickly and accurately. We can no longer afford to tolerate relatively simple security problems like those presented in this OWASP Top 10 [1].

2.1 Application Security Risks

Attackers can potentially use many different paths through application to do harm to business or organization. Each of these paths represents a risk that may, or may not, be serious enough to warrant attention [15].

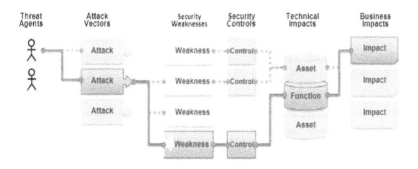

Figure-2: Flow of application security risks

Sometimes these paths are trivial to find and exploit, and sometimes they are extremely difficult. Similarly, the harm that is caused may be of no consequence, or it may put you out of business. To determine the risk to the organization, you can evaluate the likelihood associated with each threat agent, attack vector, and security weakness and combine it with an estimate of the technical and business impact to the organization. Together, these factors determine your overall risk.

Common web application vulnerabilities can be classified into three types: Injection Vulnerabilities, Business Logic Vulnerabilities and Session Management Vulnerabilities. The following diagram shows a classification of several types of attacks that are commonly used to exploit each type of vulnerability [12].

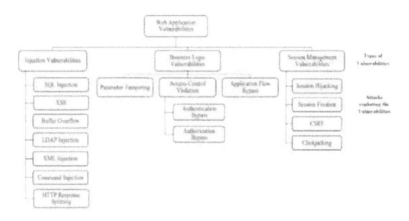

Figure-3: Web application vulnerabilities classification

Injection Vulnerabilities: An injection occurs when an attacker sends untrusted data as part of an apparently legitimate command or query in order to trick the interpreter of the application and execute unintended commands. Most common types of injections are SQL injection, Cross Site Scripting (XSS) and LDAP injection.

Business Logic Vulnerabilities: Business Logic Vulnerabilities allow malicious attackers to manipulate the legitimate logic of the application and execute illegitimate transactions. These vulnerabilities are usually exploited by modifying parameters, bypassing authentication and authorization constraints and violating the normal flow of an application.

Session Management Vulnerabilities: Session Management Vulnerabilities allow attackers to read or manipulate session variables that are used to keep the state of web applications (e.g. state that a user is logged into the application and has certain authorization rights). Session hijacking and fixation attacks target on the session ID of the user whereas Cross Site Request Forgery (CSRF) and click jacking aim the client's browser to submit requests that the legitimate user would not want to submit.

The OWASP Top 10 document [16] [17] is commonly referenced when mentioning the most common web application security flaws. The document describes the 10 most common flaws based on data collected from hundreds of organizations and over 50,000 applications and APIs, and it classifies them based on their prevalence and consensus estimates of exploitability, detectability and impact. The OWASP Top 10

8

document also gives mitigation recommendations aiming to help developers and organizations to better protect their applications. The OWASP Top 10 2013 and 2017 documents classify the top most common flaws into 10 categories that are summarized below.

OWASP Top 10 - 2013	→	OWASP Top 10 - 2017
A1 – Injection	→	A1:2017-Injection
A2 – Broken Authentication and Session Management	→	A2:2017-Broken Authentication
A3 – Cross-Site Scripting (XSS)	↘	A3:2017-Sensitive Data Exposure
A4 – Insecure Direct Object References [Merged+A7]	∪	A4:2017-XML External Entities (XXE) [NEW]
A5 – Security Misconfiguration	↘	A5:2017-Broken Access Control [Merged]
A6 – Sensitive Data Exposure	↗	A6:2017-Security Misconfiguration
A7 – Missing Function Level Access Contr [Merged+A4]	∪	A7:2017-Cross-Site Scripting (XSS)
A8 – Cross-Site Request Forgery (CSRF)	☒	A8:2017-Insecure Deserialization [NEW, Community]
A9 – Using Components with Known Vulnerabilities	→	A9:2017-Using Components with Known Vulnerabilities
A10 – Unvalidated Redirects and Forwards	☒	A10:2017-Insufficient Logging&Monitoring [NEW,Comm.]

Table-1: OWASP Top 10 2017 security flaws

The 2017 version merges previous A4 and A7 categories into a renamed "A4 – Broken Access Control" category, drops the "Invalidated Redirects and Forwards" category and introduces 2 new categories: "A7- Insufficient Attack Protection" and "A10- Under protected APIs". It is significant to note that the top three categories remain unchanged (Injection, Broken Authentication and Session Management and Cross Site Scripting (XSS) and they keep being considered as the three most important web application security flaws according to the OWASP nonprofit organization.

Information about the OWASP web application flaws categories is summarized below.

Injection:

[2] An application is vulnerable to attack when:

• User-supplied data is not validated, filtered, or sanitized by the application.

• Dynamic queries or non-parameterized calls without context aware escaping are used directly in the interpreter.

• Hostile data is used within object-relational mapping (ORM) search parameters to extract additional, sensitive records.

• Hostile data is directly used or concatenated, such that the SQL or command contains both structure and hostile data in dynamic queries, commands, or stored procedures.

Some of the more common injections are SQL, NoSQL, OS command, Object Relational Mapping (ORM), LDAP, and Expression Language (EL) or Object Graph Navigation Library (OGNL) injection. The concept is identical among all interpreters. Source code review is the best method of detecting if applications are vulnerable to injections, closely followed by thorough automated testing of all parameters, headers, URL, cookies, JSON, SOAP, and XML data inputs. Organizations can include static source (SAST) and dynamic application test (DAST) tools into the CI/CD pipeline to identify newly introduced injection flaws prior to production deployment.

Example:

Scenario #1: An application uses untrusted data in the construction of the following vulnerable SQL call:

String query = "SELECT * FROM accounts WHERE custID='" + request.getParameter("id") + "'";

Scenario #2: Similarly, an application's blind trust in frameworks may result in queries that are still vulnerable, (e.g. Hibernate Query Language (HQL)):

Query HQLQuery = session.createQuery("FROM accounts WHERE custID='" + request.getParameter("id") + "'");

In both cases, the attacker modifies the 'id' parameter value in their browser to send: ' or '1'='1. For example:

http://example.com/app/accountView?id=' or '1'='1

This changes the meaning of both queries to return all the records from the accounts table. More dangerous attacks could modify or delete data, or even invoke stored procedures.

Prevention: Preventing injection requires keeping data separate from commands and queries.

• The preferred option is to use a safe API, which avoids the use of the interpreter entirely or provides a parameterized interface, or migrate to use Object Relational Mapping Tools (ORMs). Note: Even when parameterized, stored procedures can still introduce SQL injection if PL/SQL or T-SQL concatenates queries and data, or executes hostile data with EXECUTE IMMEDIATE or exec().

• Use positive or "whitelist" server-side input validation. This is not a complete defense as many applications require special characters, such as text areas or APIs for mobile applications.

• For any residual dynamic queries, escape special characters using the specific escape syntax for that interpreter. Note: SQL structure such as table names, column names, and so on cannot be escaped, and thus user-supplied structure names are dangerous. This is a common issue in report-writing software.

• Use LIMIT and other SQL controls within queries to prevent mass disclosure of records in case of SQL injection.

Broken Authentication: [3] Confirmation of the user's identity, authentication, and session management are critical to protect against authentication-related attacks. There may be authentication weaknesses if the application:

• Permits automated attacks such as credential stuffing, where the attacker has a list of valid usernames and passwords.

• Permits brute force or other automated attacks.

• Permits default, weak, or well-known passwords, such as "Password1" or "admin/admin".

• Uses weak or ineffective credential recovery and forgot password processes, such as "knowledge-based answers", which cannot be made safe.

• Uses plain text, encrypted, or weakly hashed passwords (see A3:2017-Sensitive Data Exposure).

• Has missing or ineffective multi-factor authentication.

• Exposes Session IDs in the URL (e.g., URL rewriting).

• Does not rotate Session IDs after successful login.

• Does not properly invalidate Session IDs. User sessions or authentication tokens (particularly single sign-on (SSO) tokens) aren't properly invalidated during logout or a period of inactivity.

Example:

Scenario #1: Credential stuffing, the use of lists of known passwords, is a common attack. If an application does not implement automated threat or credential stuffing protections, the application can be used as a password oracle to determine if the credentials are valid.

Scenario #2: Most authentication attacks occur due to the continued use of passwords as a sole factor. Once considered best practices, password rotation and complexity requirements are viewed as encouraging users to use, and reuse, weak passwords. Organizations are recommended to stop these practices per NIST 800-63 and use multi-factor authentication.

Scenario #3: Application session timeouts aren't set properly. A user uses a public computer to access an application. Instead of selecting "logout" the user simply closes the browser tab and walks away. An attacker uses the same browser an hour later, and the user is still authenticated.

Prevention:

• Where possible, implement multi-factor authentication to prevent automated, credential stuffing, brute force, and stolen credential re-use attacks.

• Do not ship or deploy with any default credentials, particularly for admin users.

• Implement weak-password checks, such as testing new or changed passwords against a list of the top 10000 worst passwords.

• Align password length, complexity and rotation policies with NIST 800-63 B's guidelines in section 5.1.1 for Memorized Secrets or other modern, evidence based password policies.

• Ensure registration, credential recovery, and API pathways are hardened against account enumeration attacks by using the same messages for all outcomes.

• Limit or increasingly delay failed login attempts. Log all failures and alert administrators when credential stuffing, brute force, or other attacks are detected.

• Use a server-side, secure, built-in session manager that generates a new random session ID with high entropy after login. Session IDs should not be in the URL, be securely stored and invalidated after logout, idle, and absolute timeouts.

Sensitive Data Exposure: [4] The first thing is to determine the protection needs of data in transit and at rest. For example, passwords, credit card numbers, health records, personal information and business secrets require extra protection, particularly if that data falls under privacy laws, e.g. EU's General Data Protection Regulation (GDPR), or regulations, e.g. financial data protection such as PCI Data Security Standard (PCI DSS). For all such data:

• Is any data transmitted in clear text? This concerns protocols such as HTTP, SMTP, and FTP. External internet traffic is especially dangerous. Verify all internal traffic e.g. between load balancers, web servers, or back-end systems.

• Is sensitive data stored in clear text, including backups?

• Are any old or weak cryptographic algorithms used either by default or in older code?

• Are default crypto keys in use, weak crypto keys generated or re-used, or is proper key management or rotation missing?

• Is encryption not enforced, e.g. are any user agent (browser) security directives or headers missing?

• Does the user agent (e.g. app, mail client) not verify if the received server certificate is valid?

Example:

Scenario #1: An application encrypts credit card numbers in a database using automatic database encryption. However, this data is automatically decrypted when retrieved, allowing an SQL injection flaw to retrieve credit card numbers in clear text.

Scenario #2: A site doesn't use or enforce TLS for all pages or supports weak encryption. An attacker monitors network traffic (e.g. at an insecure wireless network), downgrades connections from HTTPS to HTTP, intercepts requests, and steals the user's session cookie. The attacker then replays this cookie and hijacks the user's (authenticated) session, accessing or modifying the user's private data. Instead of the above they could alter all transported data, e.g. the recipient of a money transfer. Scenario

#3: The password database uses unsalted or simple hashes to store everyone's passwords. A file upload flaw allows an attacker to retrieve the password database. All the unsalted hashes can be exposed with a rainbow table of pre-calculated hashes. Hashes generated by simple or fast hash functions may be cracked by GPUs, even if they were salted.

Prevention: Do the following, at a minimum, and consult the references:

• Classify data processed, stored, or transmitted by an application. Identify which data is sensitive according to privacy laws, regulatory requirements, or business needs.

• Apply controls as per the classification.

• Don't store sensitive data unnecessarily. Discard it as soon as possible or use PCI DSS compliant tokenization or even truncation. Data that is not retained cannot be stolen.

• Make sure to encrypt all sensitive data at rest.

• Ensure up-to-date and strong standard algorithms, protocols, and keys are in place; use proper key management.

• Encrypt all data in transit with secure protocols such as TLS with perfect forward secrecy (PFS) ciphers, cipher prioritization by the server, and secure parameters. Enforce encryption using directives like HTTP Strict Transport Security (HSTS).

• Disable caching for responses that contain sensitive data.

• Store passwords using strong adaptive and salted hashing functions with a work factor (delay factor), such as Argon2, scrypt, bcrypt, or PBKDF2.

• Verify independently the effectiveness of configuration and settings.

XML External Entities (XXE): [5] Applications and in particular XML-based web services or downstream integrations might be vulnerable to attack if:

• The application accepts XML directly or XML uploads, especially from untrusted sources, or inserts untrusted data into XML documents, which is then parsed by an XML processor.

• Any of the XML processors in the application or SOAP based web services has document type definitions (DTDs) enabled. As the exact mechanism for disabling DTD processing varies by processor, it is good practice to consult a reference such as the OWASP Cheat Sheet 'XXE Prevention'.

• If your application uses SAML for identity processing within federated security or single sign on (SSO) purposes. SAML uses XML for identity assertions, and may be vulnerable.

• If the application uses SOAP prior to version 1.2, it is likely susceptible to XXE attacks if XML entities are being passed to the SOAP framework.

• Being vulnerable to XXE attacks likely means that the application is vulnerable to denial of service attacks including the Billion Laughs attack.

Example: Numerous public XXE issues have been discovered, including attacking embedded devices. XXE occurs in a lot of unexpected places, including deeply nested dependencies. The easiest way is to upload a malicious XML file, if accepted:

Scenario #1: The attacker attempts to extract data from the server:

```
<?xml version="1.0" encoding="ISO-8859-1"?> <!DOCTYPE foo [ <!ELEMENT foo ANY > <!ENTITY xxe SYSTEM "file:///etc/passwd" >]> <foo>&xxe;</foo>
```

Scenario #2: An attacker probes the server's private network by changing the above ENTITY line to:

```
<!ENTITY xxe SYSTEM "https://192.168.1.1/private" >]>
```

Scenario #3: An attacker attempts a denial-of-service attack by including a potentially endless file:

```
<!ENTITY xxe SYSTEM "file:///dev/random" >]>
```

Prevention: Developer training is essential to identify and mitigate XXE. Besides that, preventing XXE requires:

• Whenever possible, use less complex data formats such as JSON, and avoiding serialization of sensitive data.

• Patch or upgrade all XML processors and libraries in use by the application or on the underlying operating system. Use dependency checkers. Update SOAP to SOAP 1.2 or higher.

• Disable XML external entity and DTD processing in all XML parsers in the application, as per the OWASP Cheat Sheet 'XXE Prevention'.

• Implement positive ("whitelisting") server-side input validation, filtering, or sanitization to prevent hostile data within XML documents, headers, or nodes.

• Verify that XML or XSL file upload functionality validates incoming XML using XSD validation or similar.

• SAST tools can help detect XXE in source code, although manual code review is the best alternative in large, complex applications with many integrations.

If these controls are not possible, consider using virtual patching, API security gateways, or Web Application Firewalls (WAFs) to detect, monitor, and block XXE attacks.

Broken Access Control: [6] Access control enforces policy such that users cannot act outside of their intended permissions. Failures typically lead to unauthorized information disclosure, modification or destruction of all data, or performing a business function outside of the limits of the user. Common access control vulnerabilities include:

• Bypassing access control checks by modifying the URL, internal application state, or the HTML page, or simply using a custom API attack tool.

• Allowing the primary key to be changed to another users record, permitting viewing or editing someone else's account.

• Elevation of privilege. Acting as a user without being logged in, or acting as an admin when logged in as a user.

• Metadata manipulation, such as replaying or tampering with a JSON Web Token (JWT) access control token or a cookie or hidden field manipulated to elevate privileges, or abusing JWT invalidation

• CORS misconfiguration allows unauthorized API access.

• Force browsing to authenticated pages as an unauthenticated user or to privileged pages as a standard user. Accessing API with missing access controls for POST, PUT and DELETE.

Example:

Scenario #1: The application uses unverified data in a SQL call that is accessing account information:

pstmt.setString(1, request.getParameter("acct"));

ResultSet results = pstmt.executeQuery( );

An attacker simply modifies the 'acct' parameter in the browser to send whatever account number they want. If not properly verified, the attacker can access any user's account.

http://example.com/app/accountInfo?acct=notmyacct Scenario

#2: An attacker simply forces browses to target URLs. Admin rights are required for access to the admin page.

http://example.com/app/getappInfo

http://example.com/app/admin_getappInfo

If an unauthenticated user can access either page, it's a flaw. If a non-admin can access the admin page, this is a flaw.

Prevention: Access control is only effective if enforced in trusted server-side code or server-less API, where the attacker cannot modify the access control check or metadata.

• With the exception of public resources, deny by default.

• Implement access control mechanisms once and re-use them throughout the application, including minimizing CORS usage.

• Model access controls should enforce record ownership, rather than accepting that the user can create, read, update, or delete any record.

• Unique application business limit requirements should be enforced by domain models.

• Disable web server directory listing and ensure file metadata (e.g. .git) and backup files are not present within web roots.

• Log access control failures, alert admins when appropriate (e.g. repeated failures).

• Rate limit API and controller access to minimize the harm from automated attack tooling.

• JWT tokens should be invalidated on the server after logout. Developers and QA staff should include functional access control unit and integration tests.

Security Misconfiguration: [7] The application might be vulnerable if the application is:

• Missing appropriate security hardening across any part of the application stack, or improperly configured permissions on cloud services.

• Unnecessary features are enabled or installed (e.g. unnecessary ports, services, pages, accounts, or privileges).

• Default accounts and their passwords still enabled and unchanged.

• Error handling reveals stack traces or other overly informative error messages to users.

• For upgraded systems, latest security features are disabled or not configured securely.
• The security settings in the application servers, application frameworks (e.g. Struts, Spring, ASP.NET), libraries, databases, etc. not set to secure values.

• The server does not send security headers or directives or they are not set to secure values.

• The software is out of date or vulnerable (see A9:2017-Using Components with Known Vulnerabilities). Without a concerted, repeatable application security configuration process, systems are at a higher risk.

Example:

Scenario #1: The application server comes with sample applications that are not removed from the production server. These sample applications have known security flaws attackers use to compromise the server. If one of these applications is the admin console, and default accounts weren't changed the attacker logs in with default passwords and takes over.

Scenario #2: Directory listing is not disabled on the server. An attacker discovers they can simply list directories. The attacker finds and downloads the compiled Java classes, which they decompile and reverse engineer to view the code. The attacker then finds a serious access control flaw in the application.

Scenario #3: The application server's configuration allows detailed error messages, e.g. stack traces, to be returned to users. This potentially exposes sensitive information or underlying flaws such as component versions that are known to be vulnerable.

Scenario #4: A cloud service provider has default sharing permissions open to the Internet by other CSP users. This allows sensitive data stored within cloud storage to be accessed.

Prevention: Secure installation processes should be implemented, including:

• A repeatable hardening process that makes it fast and easy to deploy another environment that is properly locked down. Development, QA, and production environments should all be configured identically, with different credentials used in each environment. This process should be automated to minimize the effort required to setup a new secure environment.

• A minimal platform without any unnecessary features, components, documentation, and samples. Remove or do not install unused features and frameworks.

• A task to review and update the configurations appropriate to all security notes, updates and patches as part of the patch management process (see: Using Components with Known Vulnerabilities). In particular, review cloud storage permissions (e.g. S3 bucket permissions).

• A segmented application architecture that provides effective, secure separation between components or tenants, with segmentation, containerization, or cloud security groups.

• Sending security directives to clients, e.g. Security Headers.

• An automated process to verify the effectiveness of the configurations and settings in all environments.

Cross-Site Scripting (XSS): [8] There are three forms of XSS, usually targeting users' browsers:

Reflected XSS: The application or API includes unvalidated and unescaped user input as part of HTML output. A successful attack can allow the attacker to execute arbitrary HTML and JavaScript in the victim's browser. Typically the user will need to interact with some malicious link that points to an attackercontrolled page, such as malicious watering hole websites, advertisements, or similar.

Stored XSS: The application or API stores unsanitized user input that is viewed at a later time by another user or an administrator. Stored XSS is often considered a high or critical risk.

DOM XSS: JavaScript frameworks, single-page applications, and APIs that dynamically include attacker-controllable data to a page are vulnerable to DOM XSS. Ideally, the application would not send attacker-controllable data to unsafe JavaScript APIs.

Typical XSS attacks include session stealing, account takeover, MFA bypass, DOM node replacement or defacement (such as trojan login panels), attacks against the user's browser such as malicious software downloads, key logging, and other client-side attacks.

Example:

Scenario 1: The application uses untrusted data in the construction of the following HTML snippet without validation or escaping:

(String)page+="<input   name='creditcard'   type='TEXT'   value='"   + request.getParameter("CC") + "'>";

The attacker modifies the 'CC' parameter in the browser to:

'><script>document.location='http://www.attacker.com/cgi-bin/cookie.cgi? foo='+document.cookie</script>'.

This attack causes the victim's session ID to be sent to the attacker's website, allowing the attacker to hijack the user's current session.

Note: Attackers can use XSS to defeat any automated CrossSite Request Forgery (CSRF) defense the application might employ.

Prevention: Preventing XSS requires separation of untrusted data from active browser content. This can be achieved by:

• Using frameworks that automatically escape XSS by design, such as the latest Ruby on Rails, React JS. Learn the limitations of each framework's XSS protection and appropriately handle the use cases which are not covered.

• Escaping untrusted HTTP request data based on the context in the HTML output (body, attribute, JavaScript, CSS, or URL) will resolve Reflected and Stored XSS vulnerabilities. The OWASP Cheat Sheet 'XSS Prevention' has details on the required data escaping techniques.

• Applying context-sensitive encoding when modifying the browser document on the client side acts against DOM XSS. When this cannot be avoided, similar context sensitive escaping techniques can be applied to browser APIs as described in the OWASP Cheat Sheet 'DOM based XSS Prevention'.

• Enabling a Content Security Policy (CSP) is a defense-in-depth mitigating control against XSS. It is effective if no other vulnerabilities exist that would allow placing malicious code via local file includes (e.g. path traversal overwrites or vulnerable libraries from permitted content delivery networks).

Insecure Deserialization: [9] Applications and APIs will be vulnerable if they deserialize hostile or tampered objects supplied by an attacker. This can result in two primary types of attacks:

• Object and data structure related attacks where the attacker modifies application logic or achieves arbitrary remote code execution if there are classes available to the application that can change behavior during or after deserialization.

• Typical data tampering attacks, such as access-control-related attacks, where existing data structures are used but the content is changed. Serialization may be used in applications for:

• Remote- and inter-process communication (RPC/IPC)

• Wire protocols, web services, message brokers

• Caching/Persistence

• Databases, cache servers, file systems

• HTTP cookies, HTML form parameters, API authentication tokens

Example:

Scenario #1: A React application calls a set of Spring Boot microservices. Being functional programmers, they tried to ensure that their code is immutable. The solution they came up with is serializing user state and passing it back and forth with each request. An attacker notices the "R00" Java object signature, and uses the Java Serial Killer tool to gain remote code execution on the application server.

Scenario #2: A PHP forum uses PHP object serialization to save a "super" cookie, containing the user's user ID, role, password hash, and other state:

a:4:{i:0;i:132;i:1;s:7:"Mallory";i:2;s:4:"user";
i:3;s:32:"b6a8b3bea87fe0e05022f8f3c88bc960";}

An attacker changes the serialized object to give themselves admin privileges:

a:4:{i:0;i:1;i:1;s:5:"Alice";i:2;s:5:"admin";
i:3;s:32:"b6a8b3bea87fe0e05022f8f3c88bc960";}

Prevention: The only safe architectural pattern is not to accept serialized objects from untrusted sources or to use serialization mediums that only permit primitive data types. If that is not possible, consider one of more of the following:

• Implementing integrity checks such as digital signatures on any serialized objects to prevent hostile object creation or data tampering.

• Enforcing strict type constraints during deserialization before object creation as the code typically expects a definable set of classes. Bypasses to this technique have been demonstrated, so reliance solely on this is not advisable.

• Isolating and running code that deserializes in low privilege environments when possible.

• Logging deserialization exceptions and failures, such as where the incoming type is not the expected type, or the deserialization throws exceptions.

• Restricting or monitoring incoming and outgoing network connectivity from containers or servers that deserialize.

• Monitoring deserialization, alerting if a user deserializes constantly.

Using Components with Known Vulnerabilities: [10] You are likely vulnerable:

• If you do not know the versions of all components you use (both client-side and server-side). This includes components you directly use as well as nested dependencies.

• If software is vulnerable, unsupported, or out of date. This includes the OS, web/application server, database management system (DBMS), applications, APIs and all components, runtime environments, and libraries.

• If you do not scan for vulnerabilities regularly and subscribe to security bulletins related to the components you use.

• If you do not fix or upgrade the underlying platform, frameworks, and dependencies in a risk-based, timely fashion. This commonly happens in environments when patching is a monthly or quarterly task under change control, which leaves organizations open to many days or months of unnecessary exposure to fixed vulnerabilities.

• If software developers do not test the compatibility of updated, upgraded, or patched libraries.

• If you do not secure the components' configurations (see A6:2017-Security Misconfiguration).

Example:

Scenario #1: Components typically run with the same privileges as the application itself, so flaws in any component can result in serious impact. Such flaws can be accidental (e.g. coding error) or intentional (e.g. backdoor in component). Some example exploitable component vulnerabilities discovered are:

• CVE-2017-5638, a Struts 2 remote code execution vulnerability that enables execution of arbitrary code on the server, has been blamed for significant breaches.

• While internet of things (IoT) are frequently difficult or impossible to patch, the importance of patching them can be great (e.g. biomedical devices).

There are automated tools to help attackers find unpatched or misconfigured systems. For example, the Shodan IoT search engine can help you find devices that still suffer from the Heartbleed vulnerability that was patched in April 2014.

Prevention: There should be a patch management process in place to:

• Remove unused dependencies, unnecessary features, components, files, and documentation.

• Continuously inventory the versions of both client-side and server-side components (e.g. frameworks, libraries) and their dependencies using tools like versions,

Dependency Check, retire.js, etc. Continuously monitor sources like CVE and NVD for vulnerabilities in the components. Use software composition analysis tools to automate the process. Subscribe to email alerts for security vulnerabilities related to components you use.

• Only obtain components from official sources over secure links. Prefer signed packages to reduce the chance of including a modified, malicious component.

• Monitor for libraries and components that are unmaintained or do not create security patches for older versions. If patching is not possible, consider deploying a virtual patch to monitor, detect, or protect against the discovered issue.

Every organization must ensure that there is an ongoing plan for monitoring, triaging, and applying updates or configuration changes for the lifetime of the application or portfolio.

Insufficient Logging & Monitorin: [11] Insufficient logging, detection, monitoring and active response occurs any time:

• Auditable events, such as logins, failed logins, and high-value transactions are not logged.

• Warnings and errors generate no, inadequate, or unclear log messages.

• Logs of applications and APIs are not monitored for suspicious activity.

• Logs are only stored locally.

• Appropriate alerting thresholds and response escalation processes are not in place or effective.

• Penetration testing and scans by DAST tools (such as OWASP ZAP) do not trigger alerts.

• The application is unable to detect, escalate, or alert for active attacks in real time or near real time. You are vulnerable to information leakage if you make logging and alerting events visible to a user or an attacker (see Sensitive Information Exposure).

Example:

Scenario #1: An open source project forum software run by a small team was hacked using a flaw in its software. The attackers managed to wipe out the internal source code repository containing the next version, and all of the forum contents. Although source could be recovered, the lack of monitoring, logging or alerting led to a far worse breach. The forum software project is no longer active as a result of this issue.

Scenario #2: An attacker uses scans for users using a common password. They can take over all accounts using this password. For all other users, this scan leaves only one false login behind. After some days, this may be repeated with a different password.

Scenario #3: A major US retailer reportedly had an internal malware analysis sandbox analyzing attachments. The sandbox software had detected potentially unwanted software, but no one responded to this detection. The sandbox had been producing warnings for some time before the breach was detected due to fraudulent card transactions by an external bank.

Prevention: As per the risk of the data stored or processed by the application:

• Ensure all login, access control failures, and server-side input validation failures can be logged with sufficient user context to identify suspicious or malicious accounts, and held for sufficient time to allow delayed forensic analysis.

• Ensure that logs are generated in a format that can be easily consumed by a centralized log management solutions.

• Ensure high-value transactions have an audit trail with integrity controls to prevent tampering or deletion, such as append-only database tables or similar.

• Establish effective monitoring and alerting such that suspicious activities are detected and responded to in a timely fashion.

• Establish or adopt an incident response and recovery plan, such as NIST 800-61 rev 2 or later.

There are commercial and open source application protection frameworks such as OWASP AppSensor, web application firewalls such as ModSecurity with the OWASP ModSecurity Core Rule Set, and log correlation software with custom dashboards and alerting.

Summary:

The following table provides a summary of the web application vulnerabilities mentioned in this chapter including some of their characteristics and associated attacks.

RISK	Threat Agents	Attack Vectors	Security Weakness		Impacts		Score
		Exploitability	Prevalence	Detectability	Technical	Business	
A1:2017-Injection	App Specific	EASY: 3	COMMON: 2	EASY: 3	SEVERE: 3	App Specific	8.0
A2:2017-Authentication	App Specific	EASY: 3	COMMON: 2	AVERAGE: 2	SEVERE: 3	App Specific	7.0
A3:2017-Sens. Data Exposure	App Specific	AVERAGE: 2	WIDESPREAD: 3	AVERAGE: 2	SEVERE: 3	App Specific	7.0
A4:2017-XML External Entities (XXE)	App Specific	AVERAGE: 2	COMMON: 2	EASY: 3	SEVERE: 3	App Specific	7.0
A5:2017-Broken Access Control	App Specific	AVERAGE: 2	COMMON: 2	AVERAGE: 2	SEVERE: 3	App Specific	6.0
A6:2017-Security Misconfiguration	App Specific	EASY: 3	WIDESPREAD: 3	EASY: 3	MODERATE: 2	App Specific	6.0
A7:2017-Cross-Site Scripting (XSS)	App Specific	EASY: 3	WIDESPREAD: 3	EASY: 3	MODERATE: 2	App Specific	6.0
A8:2017-Insecure Deserialization	App Specific	DIFFICULT: 1	COMMON: 2	AVERAGE: 2	SEVERE: 3	App Specific	5.0
A9:2017-Vulnerable Components	App Specific	AVERAGE: 2	WIDESPREAD: 3	AVERAGE: 2	MODERATE: 2	App Specific	4.7
A10:2017-Insufficient Logging&Monitoring	App Specific	AVERAGE: 2	WIDESPREAD: 3	DIFFICULT: 1	MODERATE: 2	App Specific	4.0

Table-2: Summary of web application vulnerabilities and related attacks

3. CONCLUSIONS

Web applications are becomes popular and have wide spread interaction medium in our daily lives. But at same point using vulnerabilities the user sensitive data also disclosed regularly. This paper surveys the different web application vulnerabilities based on the security properties that web application should preserved. However we also discussed about possible solutions those reduces chances of the occurrence of the vulnerabilities. However implementation of vulnerability mitigation solutions defend the web applications from modern threats.

At the last the new advanced security attacks are always emerging, requires the security professional to have positive security solution without putting huge number of web applications at risk.

BIBLIOGRAPHY

[1] OWASP Top Ten Project:
https://www.owasp.org/index.php/Category:OWASP_Top_Ten_Project

[2] Injection: https://www.owasp.org/index.php/Top_10-2017_A1-Injection

[3] Broken Authentication: https://www.owasp.org/index.php/Top_10-2017_A2-Broken_Authentication

[4] Sensitive Data Exposure: https://www.owasp.org/index.php/Top_10-2017_A3-Sensitive_Data_Exposure

[5] XML External Entities (XXE): https://www.owasp.org/index.php/Top_10-2017_A4-XML_External_Entities_(XXE)

[6] Broken Access Control: https://www.owasp.org/index.php/Top_10-2017_A5-Broken_Access_Control

[7] Security Misconfiguration: https://www.owasp.org/index.php/Top_10-2017_A6-Security_Misconfiguration

[8] Cross-Site Scripting (XSS): https://www.owasp.org/index.php/Top_10-2017_A7-Cross-Site_Scripting_(XSS)

[9] Insecure Deserialization: https://www.owasp.org/index.php/Top_10-2017_A8-Insecure_Deserialization

[10] Using Components with Known Vulnerabilities: https://www.owasp.org/index.php/Top_10-2017_A9-Using_Components_with_Known_Vulnerabilities

[11] Insufficient Logging & Monitoring: https://www.owasp.org/index.php/Top_10-2017_A10-Insufficient_Logging%26Monitoring

[12] G. Deepa and P. S. Thilagam, "Securing web applications from injection and logic vulnerabilities: Approaches and challenges," Information and Software Technology, no. 74, pp. 160-180, 2016.

[13] Web application: https://www.maxcdn.com/one/visual-glossary/web-application/

[14] Dafydd Stuttard, Marcus Pinto. The web application hacker's handbook. *Finding and Exploiting Security Flaws 2 Second Edition*

[15] Application Security Risks: https://www.owasp.org/index.php/Top_10-2017_Application_Security_Risks

[16] OWASP Foundation, "OWASP Top-10 2013," 2013. [Online]. Available: https://www.owasp.org/images/f/f8/OWASP_Top_10_-_2013.pdf. [Accessed June 2017].

[17] OWASP Foundation, "OWASP Top-10 2017 (Release Candidate 1)," 2017. [Online]. Available: https://github.com/OWASP/Top10/raw/master/2017/OWASP%20Top%2010%20%2020 17%20RC1-English.pdf. [Accessed June 2017].